Original title:
Tropical Days and Moonlit Nights

Copyright © 2025 Creative Arts Management OÜ
All rights reserved.

Author: George Mercer
ISBN HARDBACK: 978-1-80581-679-9
ISBN PAPERBACK: 978-1-80581-206-7
ISBN EBOOK: 978-1-80581-679-9

Mosaic of Colors at Dawn

Sunrise paints the sky in pink,
While roosters dance and cows just blink.
Parrots squawk, a feathery cheer,
As flip-flops flop, the fun is near.

Coffee brews with a sassy grind,
My breakfast plate, a feast for the mind.
Pancakes flip with a joyful thud,
As syrup pools like a golden flood.

Liquid Sunshine in a Shell

A coconut smiles with a straw so bright,
Sipping sweetness, what a delight!
Waves tickle toes, laughter is spry,
As crabs in the sand give a cheeky goodbye.

Seashells whisper with secrets to share,
While flip-flops squeak, we've no time to spare.
Ocean breezes tease wild, wild hair,
Life's like a party, here and there!

The Call of Distant Shores

The compass spins with a laugh and a grin,
Maybe we'll travel, oh where to begin?
Sunscreen slathered, we're quite the sight,
As we hunt for treasures and dance with delight.

Sandcastles rise, only to fall,
With seaweed crowns, we're kings of the hall.
The tide rolls in with a playful sweep,
As naps on the beach lure us to sleep.

Moonbeams on Mango Trees

Under starlit skies, we gather 'round,
Mangoes twinkle, a treasure found.
The night is crisp with a hint of fun,
As laughter echoes, we're never done.

Mosquitoes buzz like tiny trumpets play,
While we chase fireflies, what a wild ballet!
With a slice of fruit, we're all aglow,
As dreams float softly like clouds that flow.

Journey through Star-Studded Skies

Up above, the stars have come,
They twinkle bright, without a hum.
A coconut falls, right on my head,
I laugh and dance, should be in bed.

A parrot squawks, sharing my snack,
He snatched a chip, what a knack!
We glide on air, through giggles and cheer,
As waves tickle toes, no worry here.

Palm trees sway, with rhythm divine,
Imagine the talk, they'd sip some wine.
Under the moon, we sing off-key,
The fish join in, oh such a spree!

So here we float, in a sky of dreams,
With laughter and joy, life's not as it seems.
Stars giggle back, in a cosmic embrace,
In this playful world, we've found our place.

Glistening Sands and Enchanted Nights

On glistening sands, the crabs do parade,
In tiny top hats, they're not afraid.
They dance around with such quirky flair,
While I sip my drink, without a care.

A seal pops up, with a wink and a grin,
"Join the show!" he calls, where to begin?
Flip-flops fly, as I attempt to prance,
Only to trip, missing my chance.

The waves giggle, as the sun bows down,
Seagulls gossip, parade through town.
A treasure map leads to a burger stall,
Pirate dreams of a feast for all!

Under stars that flicker with playful glee,
The night whispers secrets only we see.
So let's raise a toast, to the clumsy delight,
In a world of laughter, all feels right!

Lush Vistas and Fading Light

In the jungle, monkeys swing,
Bananas fly, oh what a fling!
Parrots squawk, they steal a snack,
And who knew flies could wear a pack?

Palms sway gently, dance so bold,
A crab in shades, oh what a show!
The sunset spills like spilled grape juice,
I laugh so hard, I call a truce!

A Dance of Fireflies and Waves

Fireflies flicker like tiny stars,
They blink and tease, just like guitars.
Waves come crashing, a silly race,
One splash, and I'm soaked from head to waist!

Seashells gather, like gossip queens,
Chattering crabs and their silly routines.
A dolphin jumps in a goofy loop,
While seagulls join the laughing troupe!

Beneath the Canopy of Dreams

Under leaves, the critters creep,
A raccoon's snore, too loud for sleep.
Frogs croak songs no one can hear,
Oh, nature's choir, lend us an ear!

Vines entwine like a tangled tale,
A sloth hangs low, but won't turn pale.
I trip on roots, let out a shout,
And turn my capsize into a rout!

Solar Kisses and Lunar Caresses

The sun smiles wide, a golden grin,
While I burn toast; oh, where to begin?
A lizard basks, as I search for shade,
He's cool and calm, I've lost my trade!

At night, the glowworms start the show,
They twinkle like confetti, a sparkly flow.
I trip on sand, face down with flair,
Starfish laugh, and I just can't care!

Firelight and Frangipani

Under the flames, we dance so bright,
With frangipani, taking flight.
A coconut falls, oh what a sound,
Laughter erupts, joy unbound.

The night is young, the drinks are cold,
We share our stories, quite bold.
A crab joins in on our merry spree,
We're the stars of this jamboree!

Secrets Between the Coral Reefs

The fish whisper tales, oh so sly,
About the mermaid who stole a pie.
Shrimp chuckle as they pass on by,
While clams just blink, with a winked eye.

An octopus juggles shells with flair,
As dolphins spin, they twirl in air.
In the depths, the secrets abound,
With sea cucumbers all around!

Morning Mist and Evenfall's Sigh

The sun peeks in, a golden grin,
While roosters crow, the day begins.
A lazy cat stretches wide awake,
Knocking over snacks, oh what a shake!

As evening falls, the stars appear,
A firefly winks, as if to leer.
We swap our tales, of absent socks,
And giggle at the fish in frocks!

Lingering Bonfire Memories

A great big fire, sparks ignites,
We roast marshmallows, oh what delights!
With sticky fingers, we can't stop,
Our laughter echoes, a thunderous bop.

The night grows old, but not too fast,
We toast to friendships meant to last.
With tales of blunders told in glee,
Each memory a treasure, wild and free!

Stars on the Velvet Horizon

The stars above are just like fries,
They sprinkle magic in our eyes.
With every twinkle, we make a wish,
Hoping for mermaids in our fish.

The velvet sky holds secrets tight,
Like squirrels planning their fun at night.
We laugh and dance on the sandy ground,
Silly stories making us feel profound.

Laughter Beneath the Coconut Tree

A coconut fell and hit my head,
Now I'm the king of this sandy bed.
With a crown made of leaves, I'm feeling grand,
Regal and proud, I survey my land.

The parrot squawks, 'What's up with you?'
I reply, 'Just beating the morning dew!'
As laughter echoes through the warm breeze,
We giggle, dance, and do as we please.

Serenade of the Sunset Waves

The waves are singing a silly tune,
Playing tag with the glowing moon.
I tried to surf on a fluffy cloud,
But ended up face-first, feeling proud.

With seashells scattered like confetti,
We prance around, our feet all muddy.
"Look at me!" I shout with glee,
As fish join in for a dance party!

Moonlit Shadows on Sand

The shadows dance like clumsy fools,
Playing hopscotch in the cool pools.
We chase fireflies, oh what a sight,
Who knew their glow could make hearts light?

As the night whispers sweet, silly charms,
We roll in the sand, feeling no qualms.
With laughter echoing near and far,
We'll take this joy, wherever we are.

Midnight Reflections in Calm Waters

On a boat with a squeaky seat,
I tried to dance, but lost my feet.
Fish jumped up and gave a cheer,
Said, "You look silly, my dear!"

The moon shone bright, a disco ball,
We spun in circles, but I took a fall.
Now the fish all laugh and tease,
They splash around with perfect ease.

Mellow Guitar Under Starlit Skies

Strumming tunes with no clear beat,
I sang so loud, it scared a fleet.
Crabs marched by with a serious frown,
Said, "Keep it down, or we'll leave town!"

Under stars, I made a scene,
With a harmonica, I joined the dream.
Lizards tapped their tiny feet,
While I played songs, oh, so sweet!

Secrets of the Island Night

In the bushes, something stirred,
A raccoon peeked, looking absurd.
I whispered secrets to the breeze,
It giggled back, as if to tease.

Banana boats float, oh so sly,
Frogs croaked jokes, they made me cry.
Under the palms, the fun unfolds,
With coconut dreams that never get old!

Twilight's Embrace

Twilight danced with a skip and jig,
I tried to join, but did a big dig.
The bananas laughed, rolled on the ground,
Said, "Join the fun, just look around!"

Fireflies buzzed with tiny lights,
While I tripped over my own sights.
The night wore on, with giggles loud,
As I made friends with a sleeping cloud!

Serenading the Cycle of Day and Night

When the sun does stretch and yawn,
Silly birds chirp at the dawn.
They flit and fly in a playful dance,
While sleepy folks are still in a trance.

As the sun beams down with a grin,
Ice cream drips off kids' chins.
Laughter fills the market square,
While random seagulls steal your fare.

Then comes the dusk, dressed in hues,
Fireflies flirt with their glowing cues.
A cat plays with a shadow's hand,
As kids complain, "This was not planned!"

Finally, the stars peep with pride,
While crabs hide out, feeling snide.
In this merry cosmic show,
Only moonlight knows where to go.

Reflecting on the Jewel of the Coast

Beneath the palms, sun hats abound,
Someone spills a drink, kerplunk, sound!
Sandy toes and giggles share,
An ice cream truck pulls up with flair.

Seashells scatter, oh what a find,
Except the one that pinches your behind!
Kids dash about, oh what a sight,
Sticking their fingers in far too tight.

Waves tease, they swish and sway,
A beach ball pops, oh what a display!
We laugh as a seagull swoops low,
Stealing a chip with an audacious show.

Yet, in the evening, stars start to gleam,
Waves whisper tales like a sweet dream.
With giggles and snacks, we unite,
Cheerful moments under soft twilight.

Twilight Whispers Above the Shoreline

The sun dips down in ocean's embrace,
While crabs do a jig—a blurry race.
Sandcastles crumble without a fight,
As kids argue, 'Mine was better!' in delight.

The breeze carries scents of sweet fritters,
A dog sniffs a flower, gathers critters.
Moonbeams bounce off the waves so bright,
And dancers gather, lost in the night.

With giggles and songs echoing around,
A toe-tingling rhythm on the ground.
Luminescent jellyfish have their say,
While toes in the sand join the playful fray.

The night marches on with a giggly tune,
As sailors shy away from the moon.
Floating laughter fills the air with glee,
Under playful shadows, forever free.

A Journey Through Shadows and Light

Morning breaks with kooky flair,
Coffee drips, but I spill everywhere.
Right by the pool, kids jump and splash,
While adults play cards and toss some trash.

In the afternoon, the sun's a tease,
Sunscreen slapped on with vivid ease.
Glorious giggles from all sides call,
Yet someone just tripped—a grand downball!

As the sun bows low with a peachy glow,
Twilight dances, inviting the show.
Fire pits crackle with marshmallow cheer,
While some clumsy souls fall over near.

And when the stars start twinkling bright,
We toast to the fun, and all feels right.
Jokes on the dunes, echoes of delight,
In this absurd dance of day and night.

Radiant Horizons and Dusk's Embrace

The sun slips down, a big orange pie,
We chase our dreams as the seagulls fly.
Ice cream drips down onto our toes,
We laugh and dance, forget all woes.

The horizon glows, a sight so bright,
We trade our worries for endless light.
Sand casts shadows where we play,
Who knew the beach could save the day?

Stars in Our Hair, Sand in Our Hearts

We comb the beach for shells so rare,
Giggling hard as we find a pair.
Stars twinkle down, they mess our hair,
Like nature's confetti, everywhere!

With every wave, our worries fade,
In this salty bubble, we've got it made.
The moon gives a wink, what a cheeky sight,
Let's dance on the sand till the morning light!

Paradise Lost, Bliss Found

I lost my flip-flop, oh where did it go?
Dancing on one foot, putting on a show.
The palm trees chuckle, the ocean roars,
As we laugh at life on this sandy floor.

A crab joins in with its silly dance,
Looks like it's got a peculiar prance.
We're kings of the beach, so wild and free,
With shells for our crowns, as silly as can be!

Nighttime Reverie by the Bay

The night air shimmers with laughter and light,
We spot a raccoon, what a silly sight!
S'mores in our hands, sticky and sweet,
The fireflies join in, tapping their feet.

We tell spooky tales, but we giggle instead,
Who knew shadows could dance in your head?
The bay whispers secrets, a bubbly tune,
As we cackle under the watchful moon!

Conversations with the Moonlight

Under the pale light, we chat with glee,
The moon rolls its eyes, just likes to tease.
Jokes about tides and silly sea foam,
Every fish hears, they all call it home.

Stars join the laughter, they're quite a crowd,
Quipping and twinkling, unusually loud.
We share whispered secrets, silly and bright,
With giggles and chuckles, we dance through the night.

The Last Dance of the Fire Dancers

On the beach, the flames twist and spin,
A dance of the fire, where laughter begins.
One stubbed a toe; the others all laughed,
A glorious blunder—oh, what a craft!

With rhythm so wild, they twirled and leaped,
Each stumble a joke, the audience cheeps.
The embers sizzle, they crack and pop,
Dancers giggle as they nearly flop.

Celestial Dreams and Island Wishes

Beneath swaying palms, we dream of delight,
With wishes on waves and the stars shining bright.
A coconut fell—it really surprised,
Laughter erupts as we rub our eyes.

The stars overhead, they wink and they blink,
Is that a crab dancing? Oh wait, it's a drink!
Wishes in shells, they float on the breeze,
Tickling our fancies, such fun little tease.

Mysteries of the Dusk Tide

The sea murmurs secrets; can you hear the rhyme?
A crab in a tuxedo, ready for prime time.
Fish wear spectacles, quite the first show,
They giggle in bubbles, putting on a glow.

The tide pulls in giggles, the shore's full of cheer,
As snails tell tall tales, let's all gather near.
With each swoosh and splash, the night takes a bow,
For even the ocean knows laughter is how.

Fluttering Hearts in Palm Shadows

Palm fronds wave like wands of cheer,
In this sunny land, we shed our fear.
Mangoes fall, and so do my shoes,
Chasing joy, I trip over views.

Laughter echoes in the warm sea breeze,
As crabs dance by, they aim to tease.
Silly hats on heads, what a sight!
We stumble under the stars so bright.

Oasis of Whispers and Echoes

A parrot squawks in the thick, green shade,
While we sip coconuts; it's a parade!
Flip-flops flapping in a quickened race,
Trying to keep up with the monkeys' pace.

Sandcastles built, but there's a twist,
Waves crash in, and oh, how they missed!
With buckets flying, we dodge the tide,
Giggling tourists, oh what a ride!

Enchantment Beneath the Banyan Tree

Under the branches, we plan our schemes,
As squirrels plot to steal our dreams.
The sun dips low, and crickets play,
Outrageous dancing at the end of the day.

One friend stumbles, what a sight,
The moon chuckles, oh, what a night!
With fireflies joining the goofy show,
We twirl and whirl, in a lively glow.

Crystal Waters at Dawn's Arrival

Morning breaks with a splashy cheer,
Fish flip-flop, and we all steer clear.
Pancakes stack high on our sunburnt toes,
As syrup drips, everyone knows.

Water blooms like a laughing tune,
Surfboards ready, we'll conquer the moon!
With waves so playful, we all collide,
Sardines in swimsuits, it's quite the ride!

The Chorus of the Night Sky

Stars giggle in the azure sheet,
Crabs dance, on joyful little feet.
Coconuts chuckle, swinging near,
While moonbeams toast with cans of beer.

Parrots squawk, with voices loud,
As dolphins leap, they join the crowd.
With a wink, the night grows bright,
Shining laughter fills delight.

Laughter echoes, secrets shared,
Under the palms, no one is scared.
Breezes tease and tickle, too,
With whispers that make you go 'Woohoo!'

So grab your snacks, let's have a feast,
A night like this, we love the least!
With silly hats and funky tunes,
We dance between the laughing dunes.

Midnight Hues of Magic Moments

Under the moon's tinfoil glow,
Laughter bubbles, just like a show.
Jellyfish giggle in the sea,
While crickets sing in harmony.

A twist of fate, a dance so strange,
While waves crash with a fun exchange.
Fireflies flicker like tiny jesters,
Offering joy, as nighttime testers.

Breezes spin in playful ways,
Making trouble on starry bays.
With each step, the sand goes squish,
Dining al fresco, oh what a dish!

So grab your friends and raise a cheer,
For magic moments, we hold dear.
With every laugh and silly fight,
The world spins wild in pure delight.

Land of Soft Indulgence

Swaying palms with sweet embrace,
Finding joy at every place.
Rum drinks served with silly names,
Under the sun, we're all the same.

Fluffy clouds wear puffball hats,
While silly monkeys strike their chats.
Feet in sand, like butter's melt,
In this paradise, so deeply felt.

Coconuts roll in laughter's game,
As playful fish do the same old claim.
Chasing sunsets, racing time,
Oh, what a joy this life can rhyme!

So welcome, friend, to blissful lands,
Where every smile just expands.
Pineapple hats upon our heads,
In this paradise, we've made our beds.

Golden Light Through Ocean Spray

Sunshine bounces off the waves,
While silly sharks become our knaves.
Board shorts flapping in the breeze,
Let's make waves, if you please!

With each splash, the laughter grows,
Tickled toes in salty flows.
Seagulls play their cheeky tricks,
As beach balls soar with silly flicks.

Casts of nets by sun-bright kids,
Finding treasure—oops, that's a squid!
Butterflies dance with flip-flop glee,
In this splashy jubilee.

So let's toast to frothy dunes,
And whistle tunes to silly tunes.
With golden light and ocean's sway,
We'll cherish laughter every day.

Whispers of the Ocean Breeze

Seagulls squawk in the sun,
While sandy toes start to run.
Crabs dance in their little shoes,
Playing games the ocean brews.

Flip-flops slap with a loud cheer,
As waves giggle, drawing near.
Beach balls bounce like happy thoughts,
In this place where laughter's caught.

The sun slips down, a golden glide,
As ice cream drips, we run, we slide.
A dolphin hiccups, leaps with flair,
Reminding us to not a care.

Under skies of watermelon hue,
We toast with drinks, a bubbly brew.
Just watch the brown crabs wave goodbye,
As we all laugh and giggle high.

Love Under Starlit Palms

Palm fronds sway like silly dancers,
While we share our sweet romances.
Bug spray sprays in clouds so thick,
Yet we laugh, the moment's slick.

Under stars that wink and jest,
We share our dreams and take a rest.
Mosquito bites can't dash our fun,
For we're in love, two hearts as one.

A coconut drops, a comical thud,
While we giggle in sand and mud.
With every drink, we're feeling bold,
To toast to rumors we've been told.

So let's twirl 'neath glowing skies,
And catch the clouds with our wild eyes.
In this love, we find delight,
As the world spins in soft moonlight.

Sunset Serenade

The sun winks low, a cheeky gleam,
As seagulls laugh, it feels like a dream.
Splashing waves hum a silly tune,
While jellyfish dance, beneath the moon.

Bikini-clad friends take a daring dip,
Laughter bubbles, a joyful trip.
Hot dogs fly, a beachside show,
As kids run wild, with energy to blow.

The sky ignites in orange and pink,
While surfboards tumble and glasses clink.
Barbecue smoke wafts with cheer,
As friends sip fizzy drinks right here.

So raise your voice, let laughter ring,
Join the fun that sunsets bring.
For every shade, a smile bright,
In this laughter filled delight.

The Lullaby of Coconut Trees

Coconuts drop with a puff and crash,
While squirrels jump like a wild splash.
Chasing shadows, we play hide and seek,
With laughter echoing, all week.

The breeze whispers tales of the day,
As pineapple hats lead us astray.
Dancing under the starry dome,
In this silly place we call home.

Beneath the trees, the grown-ups sip,
While kids go zoom on an ice-cream trip.
Sticky fingers and giggles loud,
As we dream of adventures, feeling proud.

So let your heart switch to silly tune,
And sway with the stars and the glowing moon.
In laughter's embrace, we find our peace,
With every moment, the joy won't cease.

Glimmers of Dawn on Ocean Skin

The sun peeks out, a sleepy face,
Waves tickle toes in a joyful race.
Seagulls squawk their morning cheer,
As I trip on flip-flops, oops, dear!

Pineapple juice spills on my lap,
I dance like a crab—what a strange clap!
The ocean winks with a bubbly grin,
As sand in my shorts makes me spin.

High tides come with a foam-filled laugh,
While I chase the waves, it's quite the gaffe.
But each splash is met with giggling delight,
As I frolic and play, from morning to night.

So laugh with the sea, let your worries drift,
In a world where the sun and the tide gift.
With every sparkling glow on my skin,
I know that the fun is about to begin!

The Paintbox of a Setting Sun

The sky's a painter, wild and bold,
Streaks of orange and pink unfold.
I watch the colors spill and splash,
While bees make plans for a final dash.

The coconut tree leans, takes a peek,
As I trip on roots, oh, so unique!
With laughter ringing through the air,
I chase the sunset without a care.

While shadows grow and crickets croon,
My dance brings giggles beneath the moon.
In this colorful mess, I twirl and sway,
For every sunset leads to a playful ballet.

So let the hues wrap you tight,
As we'll snack on laughter with all our might.
In this vast canvas, we'll find our way,
With mirth painting memories day after day!

Embrace of Warm Winds and Cool Nights

The warm wind whispers, a playful tease,
As palm fronds sway with a gentle breeze.
I build a fortress of sand so grand,
Till a rogue wave giggles and makes it bland.

Stars pop out like fireworks bright,
While I stumble on dreams, almost out of sight.
With friends in tow, we crack open a snack,
As fireflies join the giggly pack.

The night sky plays hide and seek,
While I attempt a dance, oh so bleak.
With laughter echoing through the trees,
I forget my worries in this cool ease.

So join me under this twinkling dome,
In a land where we make our silly home.
With fun in the air and love in each sight,
We'll savor each moment until morning light!

A Mosaic of Color and Sound

The market buzzes with flavors so bold,
As laughter and chatter, like magic, unfold.
I trip on mangoes, what a sight!
As everyone giggles at my clumsy flight.

Bamboo flutes play a tune, oh so sweet,
While I sway to rhythms with happy feet.
Each patch of color tells a tale,
Of weavings and spices that seldom fail.

The parrot squawks, "Hello, dear friend!",
As I toss it a chip, hoping it'll blend.
It cackles loud, with a cheeky grin,
As we both enjoy this curious din.

So let's paint our world with joy and cheer,
In this vivid dream, hold laughter near.
With every sound, and every hue,
We'll dance through life, just me and you!

The Soundtrack of Summer Evenings

The sun has set, the fireflies dance,
With giggles shared at every chance.
The ice cream melts, and so does the cake,
We slip on sand and jump in the lake.

The moonlit sky plays tunes so sweet,
A band of frogs joins our little feat.
A crab scuttles by with a wink of an eye,
As we sing silly songs and laugh till we cry.

The stars are out, like popcorn in air,
We'll shout out our dreams, without a care.
A breeze whispers jokes that make us all grin,
In this summer concert, let the fun begin!

The night grows older, but we stay awake,
Telling tall tales about the fish we'll create.
With a splash and a cheer, our laughter ignites,
On this carefree stage of our summer nights.

Chasing Shadows in Paradise

Under the palms, our shadows collide,
We dodge the sun with giggles and slides.
A turtle named Steve joins our parade,
He takes a slow step; we all get delayed.

The beach ball flies, we dive and we roll,
Chasing those shadows—oh, that's our goal!
A crab gives a wave, and we wave back, too,
He's quite the dancer in his own little shoe.

With buckets of sand and piles of delight,
We sculpt the world by the break of twilight.
A foam-covered wave gives a teasing poke,
And the sandcastle tumbles—oh, what a joke!

But laughter's a wave that can never be tamed,
We'll build it anew, it's never the same.
With silly canvases and smiles so bright,
We keep on creating till we say goodnight.

Flickers of Light on Still Waters

The moon takes a dip with a wink on the lake,
As we toss little pebbles, ripples we make.
A fish jumps high, wearing scales of surprise,
Flashing us smiles as it leaps to the skies.

The night unfolds, with giggles and splashes,
We race with reflections and "whoosh!" our heart crashes.

A frog in a top hat croaks out a cheer,
While a firefly joins, lighting up the sphere.

With shadows that waltz under twinkling stars,
We whisper our secrets, not caring who's far.
A splash in the air, watch the catfish strut,
Who knew that ponds could be this much fun?

So here we remain, as the laughter rings,
With flickers of light, oh, the joy that it brings!
With winks from the night, we'll dance till it's dawn,
This lake of pure magic, forever our song.

Crickets' Chorus at Dusk

The sun sinks low, the crickets come out,
Making music that we cannot live without.
A grasshopper jumps, just to join in the show,
While we swing on swings, going to and fro.

The scent of sweet food fills the warm air,
Who's got the chips? We'll all gladly share!
With smiles on our faces and popcorn in sight,
We munch and we crunch, what a marvelous night!

A squirrel peeks in, checking for crumbs,
"Did someone say snacks?" Oh, here he comes!
With laughter and cheers, we invite him to stay,
In this concert of twilight, we dance and we play.

So let the crickets keep their joyful refrain,
With each silly note, we'll giggle again.
As dusk wraps us close in its cozy embrace,
We'll sing with the stars in this perfect place.

Charms of the Nocturnal Breeze

The breeze whispers soft, oh what a tease,
As crabs dance around like they own the seas.
A parrot squawks jokes in the moonlit hue,
While the fish laugh along as they swim in a queue.

Backyard parties rock with a feel so grand,
In hammock lounges, we take our stand.
A light-up coconut rolls to my feet,
Heats up the scene with a comical beat.

Fireflies join, twinkling all around,
Each flicker a giggle, a spark, a sound.
We dance like the waves, just wild and free,
Our laughter a chorus, as wild as can be.

The stars wear a grin, they twinkle and glow,
A serenade sung by the steady ebb flow.
In a world so bright, we're the punchline bold,
Each night a new story, a memory to hold.

Dreams at the Waters' Edge

Sandy castles rise with a blink and a flinch,
Seagulls pick jokes from the beach with a clinch.
We splash in the waves, oh, what a parade,
While the crabs judge our skills, they sway and degrade.

Flip-flops in hand, we race to the shore,
Trip over our dreams and crash with a roar.
A flip of a fish breaks our laughter in twain,
As we wobble like jelly, then giggle in vain.

The tide's rhythm laughs, tickling our toes,
Chasing each wave like a game full of pros.
But one big splash sends us all airborne,
Wipe-outs aplenty, our dignity worn!

As the sun dips low, we crown a beach king,
With shells as his throne, let the laughter ring.
Dreams wash ashore, caught in seaweed webs,
We'll craft a new tale as we dance with the ebb.

Whims of a Coconut King

In a land where coconuts wear crowns of green,
Lives the Coconut King with a wit so keen.
He juggles his fruits, not a single one drops,
While the birds chirp tunes, doing little hop hops.

His throne made of shells, quite quirky and grand,
He calls for a feast with the wave of his hand.
The parrots provide jokes that never fall flat,
As monkeys bring snacks like a little wild chat.

With laughter, he dances under bright shiny stars,
Waving to elephants rolling by in their cars.
A minion of crabs plays the drums by the shore,
Each beat brings us joy, let's party some more!

But don't tie him down, let him roam with the breeze,
For this king of the island turns work into tease.
With each carefree chuckle, he sparkles like dew,
Making whims of the night dance, spontaneous and new.

Driftwood Tales Under Starlight

On the soft sands, driftwood tales come alive,
As the tide joins in, it starts to connive.
With a lantern of laughter, we gather around,
Every twist of the wood brings new stories profound.

A pirate once found a hat made of shells,
Claimed it brought fortune with hilarious yells.
His parrot would squawk, "Opt for more bling!"
As the night wrapped us up in the tales that they bring.

From fish that wear shoes to crabs in a band,
Their concerts a riot, bringing joy to the sand.
With each passing tide, our giggles reprise,
Under starlit confetti, we spark new highs.

So raise up a cup, let the laughter unfold,
As we share spin tales, both goofy and bold.
The driftwood stands guard, our secrets it keeps,
While the moon winks down, as the whole island sleeps.

Sweet Currents in the Evening Breeze

The parrot shouts a joke so loud,
While I sip rum under a small cloud.
A coconut falls, it hits my hair,
I laugh so hard, I spill my flair.

Chasing crabs that scuttle fast,
With little legs, they run and gasp.
I slip and fall on sand so soft,
A seagull laughs, it takes off aloft.

The sun dips low, the sky's a show,
Shades of pink, with a twist of glow.
I dance with shadows, feet in the tub,
While my friend tries to steal my grub.

A gentle breeze plays with my drink,
My thoughts float high, not on the brink.
As I share this silly scene,
Life's a beach, it's like a dream!

Fragrant Nights Under the Stars

The moon hums softly, a funny tune,
While I munch on tacos under a maroon.
A breeze brings scents of spicy stew,
    I spill my salsa, oh what a view!

With stars like glitter, some dance in place,
    A firefly's waltz, it's quite the race.
We try to catch them, fall on the grass,
    And giggle at whispers from the sass.

A lizard peers, curious as can be,
    As I squeak jokes, feeling so free.
We toast with drinks that bubble and fizz,
    To nights like this, oh what a whiz!

With laughter ringing, the moon blinks low,
    I chase the breeze, with antics aglow.
These fragrant nights hold stories untold,
    In giggles and glee, our lives unfold.

When the Ocean Calls Our Names

The waves whisper secrets, a cheeky surprise,
While seagulls cackle and dive from the skies.
I build a sandcastle made of dreams,
But it collapses! Oh, how it seems!

With buckets in hand, we roam the shore,
Retelling tales of ocean folklore.
Crabs in a line, a silly parade,
I wish I could join, but I'm really dismayed.

The fish in the tide wiggle and squirm,
I joke they wish for a life long-term.
They peek and they poke, oh such a sight,
As I slip on the seaweed, oh what a fright!

Our laughter mingles with salt in the air,
As we moonwalk through puddles without any care.
When the ocean hums, it plays our song,
In waves of joy, where we all belong.

The Lightness of Being in Paradise

With flip-flops squeaking, we sway to the beat,
The sun winks down, oh what a treat!
A funny hat blows off with the breeze,
And suddenly, I'm dressed like a tease!

Pineapple drinks with tiny umbrellas,
We giggle at folks dressed like fella's.
The rhythms of laughter fill the air,
As we imitate a crab with flair.

Under palm fronds, we dance with glee,
A monkey chuckles, he's watching me.
He swings and he twirls, I give him a wave,
In this lightness, it's joy we crave.

With sun on our skin, we bask and we play,
As night paints the sky, it ends the day.
But in our hearts, we'll keep this bliss,
In giggles and glee, we'll never miss.

Echoes of the Gentle Tide

The ocean hums a silly tune,
As crabs do a jig beneath the moon.
The waves are laughing, can't you see?
Even fish roll their eyes in glee.

Seagulls squawk with comedic flair,
While coconuts drop without a care.
Palm trees sway, they've lost their groove,
Dancing awkwardly, trying to move.

Starfish wear hats, so fancy and bright,
They hold a party every night.
And if you listen, you might find,
The shells are gossiping, oh so unkind!

So grab a drink with an umbrella,
Join this bizarre beach fella.
The tide will waltz, then trip on sand,
A comedy show that's simply grand!

Celestial Dance on Coral Shores

The moon wears shades, it's quite a sight,
Winking at fish in the dead of night.
Crabs form a conga line with flair,
They shuffle sideways without a care.

Stars twinkle like a disco ball,
While turtles try to have a ball.
Shells are the audience, glued to the fun,
Murmuring jokes, till the morn has begun.

Laughter echoes through the salty air,
The dolphins mimic—what a pair!
Breezes tickle the beachside sand,
As if the night had made a plan.

The sandcastles giggle, quite absurd,
As waves crash in, they're not deterred.
In this paradise of whimsy and cheer,
Every night's magic, don't you fear!

The Enchantment of Warm Evenings

Fireflies dance like little stars,
Buzzing about in silly cars.
They zigzag past a sleepy cat,
Who ponders if they might be snacks.

A coconut falls! Oh what a sight,
It rolls away, somewhere out of sight.
Laughter fills the balmy air,
As friends share tales with playful flair.

In hammocks hung between palm trees,
Laughter sways with the gentle breeze.
Watermelons giggle on picnic spreads,
As jokes bounce off all the sleepy heads.

The sun dips down, paints skies with glee,
As laughter echoes, wild and free.
Each warm evening, a comedy spree,
Under the stars, just you and me!

Passionate Breezes and Hidden Shores

In the cool of dusk, a breeze does tease,
Whispering secrets through the trees.
Laughter hides where the shadows play,
As crickets chirp in a funny way.

Sneaky waves tickle the sandy toes,
Creating giggles as the wind blows.
An octopus waves, wearing a tie,
While seashells shout, "Just give it a try!"

The stars play tag above the way,
Making wishes on this balmy day.
Every breeze brings a playful jest,
Nature's comedy, simply the best.

So join the fun, take a chance,
Where anything can lead to a dance.
In hidden nooks by shorelines bright,
The laughter echoes throughout the night!

Silhouettes Against a Golden Glow

Sunburned toes in the sand,
Flip-flops lost, I panicked and ran.
Laughter echoes in the air,
Seagulls steal my chips with flair.

Umbrellas dance, a silly sight,
Someone's hat takes off in flight.
Beach balls bounce, a playful game,
While my sunscreen forgot my name.

Shells and laughter, a perfect blend,
My buddy's lost, but he'll pretend.
Waves invite us for a swim,
But first, let's see who's lost a limb!

Setting sun gives quite the show,
As crabs scuttle – stealing the glow.
We raise a toast to fun-filled days,
While the ocean swirls in a silly haze.

A Symphony of Salt and Sky

A coconut drops, bonk on the head,
Spicy fish tacos – a feast instead!
Mermaids giggle at our grand mischief,
We sing off-key, just to be brief.

Kites soar high, tangled in trees,
Insect choruses hum like bees.
Someone's sandals, a fashion statement,
While my drink spills - call it a lament.

Surfboards wobble, we take our stance,
Mission to surf ends in a dance.
Salt in my hair, sand in my drink,
Taking a dip, but barely we sink!

Pirates laugh as they steal our fries,
Chasing gulls under candy skies.
With a wink, we dive in for a wave,
Another round of shenanigans to rave.

The Breath of Warm Winds

Warm breezes toss my hair like a mop,
A crab skitters by, should I stop?
Tanning lotion – missing the boat,
Sipping a drink that tastes like a goat!

Friends play limbo, a wild affair,
One goes too low, but who can bare?
Laughter and splashes join in the fun,
While a beach ball flies, oh, what a run!

Sunburned noses and tired eyes,
Joking about mermaids with wigs and lies.
Fish tacos dance in shiny wraps,
Count how many pies fit in our laps.

With every gust, we sway side by side,
Fish stories traded, we can't abide.
The day winds down, the party ignites,
As sandcastles crumbled, we call it a night.

Embrace of Silver Seashells

With seashells tucked in my pocket deep,
Seagulls chortle – a secret to keep.
Crabs march by with their painted shells,
While I giggle at my sandy spells.

Sunsets painting the skies with flair,
A sand dog howls, caught unaware.
Building castles, a grand design,
Only for waves to think it's divine.

We challenge the tide, who will win?
Wet feet dancing, soaked to the chin!
Sun tired out, gives way to nights,
Bags filled with laughter, joyful heights.

Beneath the stars, nonsense takes flight,
As shadows leap in the warm moonlight.
With candy and laughter, we simply flee,
Embracing the thrill of the salty sea.

Ebb and Flow of a Starry Night

The waves are laughing, oh so loud,
They wear a shimmering, silvery shroud.
The crabs are dancing, what a sight,
Even the moon is laughing tonight.

A fish tried flying, oh what a flop,
But the seagulls giggle, they just can't stop.
Stars wink at secrets, whispers of cheer,
As jellyfish juggle—let's give them a beer!

Sandcastles tumble with the breeze,
Shells play tag while the palm trees tease.
Under the laughter of night's gentle glow,
The ocean tells tales, wouldn't you know?

So let's raise our drinks, with ice and a twist,
To this quirky night we cannot resist.
For in this wild, whimsical parade,
Friendship and joy are unafraid.

Reflections of the Gentle Dawn

The sun peeks out, with a sleepy yawn,
While roosters crow about the lawn.
A squirrel sips coffee, looking quite smug,
And turtles chuckle, hiding in a rug.

Waves play tag with the soft, wet sand,
As flip-flops tangling goes unplanned.
The seagulls gossip, getting their fill,
In this silly scene, time stands still.

Old crabs tell stories, both tall and grand,
While bright fish swim in a synchronized band.
Reflections shimmer, a wobbly show,
As nature cracks jokes, what a humorous flow!

So grab a smoothie, let laughter bloom,
Under the sun, we dance and zoom.
A day full of giggles awaits in the glow,
Let's embrace the chuckles that joyfully flow.

Coconut's Whisper in the Breeze

A coconut rolls down a sandy street,
Chasing the crabs with tiny quick feet.
The breeze carries laughter, a comical tune,
While leaves join in, swaying to the moon.

A parrot shouts jokes from high on a tree,
As surfers laugh, feeling so free.
The tide comes in with a wink and a grin,
As flip-flops go missing, let the chaos begin!

Bananas take turns sliding with flair,
While pineapples gossip, without a care.
Rice paddies giggle at their strange friends,
As cacti dream up comical ends.

So let's toast a coconut, let smiles increase,
For laughter and joy make the world a feast.
In this fruity affair, where silliness thrives,
Every moment is golden, as fun comes alive.

Luminescent Tales of the Shore

The shoreline sparkles, a magical sight,
With sandcastles glowing in the twilight.
A starfish in sequins offers a dance,
While crabs swing by, enjoying their chance.

The moonlight winks, it's quite the tease,
As jellybeans giggle and bounce in the breeze.
Sea turtles gossip, telling tall tales,
While fish wear sunglasses, no need for scales!

Waves trade whispers, bubbling with cheer,
In this whimsical world, there's nothing to fear.
And under the stars, the giggles ignite,
A balmy breeze brings dreams to the night.

So join in the laughter, let spirits soar,
In this luminescent playground by the shore.
Where stories come alive with a glimmering glow,
And the essence of fun continues to flow.

The Magic of Still Waters at Dawn

Waking up at dawn's first light,
My hair's a mess, but that's alright.
Coffee spills while I take a sip,
Falling back, I take another trip.

The fish are jumping, what a sight!
They tease me as they take their flight.
A duck swims by with a cheeky grin,
I can't help but let the laughter in.

A frog croaks loudly, what a croon,
He thinks he's quite the maestro tune.
I wave goodbye to my sleepy woes,
As the sun climbs high, the merriment flows.

The still waters reflect my glee,
Potato sack races just for me.
With silly hats and silly games,
We splash around, no one to blame.

Ebb and Flow of Dreams and Reality

The waves roll in, with winks and winks,
As I drift and ponder, then overthink.
Caught in a daydream, I misplace my shoe,
Now covered in sand, my toes go 'boo-hoo!'

Reality bites, then turns to a laugh,
I build a grand castle, it's more of a chaff.
A pigeon swoops down to claim my crown,
Looks like this king's gonna wear a frown!

People stroll by, they shake their heads,
Who's this mad poet, dreaming in spreads?
But I just grin while I play in the foam,
With seaweed pals, I'm never alone!

As the tide pulls back, I twirl and spin,
Posing for selfies, let the fun begin!
Ephemeral moments, we hold them tight,
In this dance of dreams, we take flight.

Whispers of the Ocean Breeze

The ocean breeze whispers, soft and sly,
It tickles my ear and makes me fly.
A seagull squawks, claiming the throne,
While I try to steal its snack—what a bone!

With sandy toes, I dance on the shore,
Dropping my fries, who could ask for more?
Now battling a crab, it's a showdown fierce,
That pinch was close, it's making me pierce!

The sun plays peek-a-boo with the trees,
As I chase a leaf carried by the breeze.
Why does everything run away from me?
It's just a crab, and it's time for tea!

Laughter ensues, the day drifts on,
With every quirk, a new comic dawn.
Twinkling sprites in the sparkle of waves,
Make me a fool, but it's fun that saves!

Lanterns in the Palm Canopy

Under the palms, the lanterns glow,
Like fireflies caught in a dreamy show.
I trip over roots, my dance is wild,
Like a clumsy elf, nature's own child.

The chatter of crickets fills the air,
As I strut and stumble without a care.
A coconut drops, rolls under my feet,
I bounce like a ball, take that on repeat!

The stars above join in the game,
Whispering secrets that spark my flame.
In every laugh, I hear a new tune,
While the moon looks down, grinning at June.

So here we sway, in this vibrant night,
With lanterns aglow, we dance till first light.
A merry mishap, it's pure delight,
Under the palms, everything feels right!

Dance of the Fireflies at Dusk

Tiny lights flicker in play,
Bouncing like kids at the end of the day.
They twirl and swirl, oh what a sight,
Like tiny fairies in the fading light.

A ladybug joins, trying to cope,
Wobbling around with no sense of hope.
But fireflies giggle, they shine and flit,
While the snail just grumbles, 'I can't keep fit!'

The stars peek out, feeling quite shy,
As crickets hum their nightly lullaby.
The moon chuckles softly, glowing so bright,
Saying, 'Who knew bugs could dance with such might?'

Just as the night paints a magical scene,
A cat jumps in, acting all mean.
But all the fireflies, in a daring line,
Danced right past it, oh how divine!

Echoes of the Evening Tide

The waves come crashing with a roar,
While seagulls laugh, not caring for shore.
A crab waves hello with its little claw,
While swimmers shout, 'Oh! What a flaw!'

A dolphin does flips, quite out of sync,
Splashing folks nearby with a cheeky wink.
The beach ball drifts, caught in a slide,
While sunscreen battles the tide with pride.

The sunset spills colors, a vibrant sight,
A painter's dream, so full of delight.
"Hey, grab your sandals!" someone will shout,
As the tide tickles toes, and fears cast out.

With sandy hair and laughter loud,
We dance on the shore, feeling so proud.
The echoes of joy, like a catchy tune,
As the ocean sings to the rising moon.

Raindrops on Hibiscus Petals

Pitter-patter starts the fun,
As blooms giggle in the sun.
Raindrops slide, a slippery sight,
Hibiscus blush in pure delight.

A frog croaks, searching for flies,
While the petals wear tiny sighs.
"Dance with me!" the raindrops plead,
As they twirl on flowers with glee indeed.

But a bee buzzes in, oh so bold,
Hoping to find some nectar gold.
"Hey! You're wrecking my flower parade!"
The hibiscus grumbles, slightly dismayed.

But laughter bubbles as they all play,
Nature's troops in a comical sway.
As the sun peeks back, the raindrops flee,
Leaving behind joy for all to see.

Swaying Palms and Gentle Dreams

Palms are swaying, taking a rest,
While breezes dance, really the best.
A monkey swings with a cheeky grin,
As coconuts roll - oh where have they been?

A parrot squawks, 'Let's start a band!'
While the nightingale joins, so sweet and grand.
They sing to the stars, while the lizards tap,
Creating a show, no one's heard of that!

The shadows play tricks, making things bend,
As the moonlit glow sets the mood to blend.
"Stay with us!" the stars twinkle bright,
While the ocean hums its lullaby tonight.

With dreams swirling high like a warm sea breeze,
It tickles our hearts, puts our minds at ease.
Under the palms, where laughter's the theme,
We sway to the rhythm of whimsical dreams.

Midnight Tide and Lantern Glow

The crabs are having a fancy ball,
With tiny tuxedos, standing tall.
Dancing on sand under starlit beams,
While seagulls plot their nighttime schemes.

Umbrellas flipped, what a sight to see,
Don't dare let your drink fall into the sea!
The ocean laughs at our silly plight,
As we trip and tumble into the night.

A beach ball bounces, the laughter flies,
With jellyfish that just want to rise.
They wiggle and giggle in the swirling tide,
With every misstep, oh what a ride!

We gather seashells, well, sort of, you know,
They keep running away, what a wild show!
But in this chaos, we couldn't care less,
For lanterns keep glowing, our beachside fest!

Sand Between Our Toes

We skipped along with flip-flops in hand,
Only to find we're stuck in the sand.
Each step we take leads to sandy woes,
But oh, the laughter when no one knows!

Sipping coconut drinks with a funny straw,
Mimicking toucans and their funny jaw.
With every sip, the straws all go shloop,
It's a party with each sandy scoop!

Seagulls are thieves on a snatching spree,
They've taken our chips, oh can't you see?
Yet here we are, sand covered and fine,
With salt on our lips, we continue to dine.

We build a castle, quite the masterpiece,
But ocean waves crash, it's a quick release!
As we splash and tumble, the sun starts to set,
These silly memories, I'll never forget!

Secrets of the Midnight Surf

The waves are whispering secrets tonight,
Sharing tales of mischief, laughter, and fright.
A dolphin jumps in with a splashing cheer,
While we try to juggle, oh what a sight here!

The ocean's got jokes and we're all the punchline,
As fish swim around in a stylish design.
With glow-in-the-dark fins, they dance with glee,
While we slurp on snacks from our picnic spree!

Who needs a party when you've got the tide?
In a game of tag, we stumble and slide.
But wait, here comes a wave, it's coming in fast,
Just when we thought these breezy jokes last!

We laugh as we're soaked, our faces aglow,
For midnight mischief is stealing the show.
Waves crash with giggles, the night is our friend,
And secrets of surf bring a night without end!

Moonbeams on a Sapphire Sea

The moon peeks down, what a cheeky grin,
While we fail at fishing, yet giggle within.
Each splash from the line sends us into fits,
It's a comedy show, with no fishing hits!

As sea turtles flip in a slow-motion race,
With grace and with laughter, they pick up the pace.
We cheer them on, can't hold in our glee,
While a crab steals our snacks — oh where could it be?

The stars are our audience, twinkling with joy,
As we balance on surfboards, not a clue, oh boy!
Tripping on waves, we fall in with a splash,
Our midnight ballet, an unplanned crash!

Yet on this sapphire sea, all is so bright,
As laughter and fun fill up the night.
With moonlit reflections and smiles galore,
We'll dance like the waves, forever, encore!

Nostalgic Lyrics of the Sea

The gulls sing loud, a crazy tune,
They steal my chips, oh, what a boon.
The waves dance bright, like a wobbly jig,
I slip on sand, oh, it's so big.

A crab in shades, he scuttles by,
He shares my snack, I can't deny.
With each splash, I just can't resist,
A summer folly, too good to miss.

The sunburn's red, my nose a sight,
I wear my hat, but it's too tight.
The tide rolls in, and here I sway,
In wet flip-flops, I lose my way.

A mermaid's laugh floats on the breeze,
I trip on shells and stumble with ease.
But laughter's bright, as waves retreat,
Each silly fall, it's purest sweet.

Bliss among the Hammocks

In a hammock made for napping bliss,
I rock too hard, I might just miss.
With juice in hand, I sip with glee,
A nearby squirrel eyes my spree.

The breeze goes whoosh, my hat takes flight,
Chasing it down feels just so right.
I twist, I turn, I leap, I flop,
Just watch the sun melt, then I stop.

My friend comes by, a playful poke,
We laugh aloud, I almost choke.
The clouds drift by, they need a nap,
We join their fluffs in a cozy wrap.

As sunset fades, we share a grin,
The dusk invites some games to spin.
Our laughter echoes, the stars take stage,
In this silly rapture, we feel no age.

Radiance of a Lasting Kiss

The moon's a cheeky, glowing pie,
It beams at me, oh me, oh my.
With each warm breeze, my hair's a mess,
I giggle soft, in this sweet dress.

A mishap here, a stumble there,
I blush as crickets whisper fair.
The tide rolls up, like a cheeky tease,
It drenches my toes with a playful wheeze.

Yet laughter leads on this shining path,
Through sandy spills and silly math.
For every slip, a snort or squeal,
These moonlit nights, they spin and reel.

Under stars, our hearts align,
In this silly dance, all will be fine.
With giggles bright, we'll chase our dreams,
In every laugh, the magic beams.

Gaze of the Serene Waters

The lake reflects a wobbly face,
I make a splash, it's a clumsy grace.
My friend beside me, with wide-eyed cheer,
Last time we fished, we caught a tear.

With poles in hand, we're ready to go,
But oops, they're tangled, oh don't you know?
A fish swims by, it gives a wink,
While we just trifle and play and stink.

We toss some bait, it hits my shoe,
Did it just bite? Oh, who knew?
With every giggle, the ripples swirl,
In this calm ease, I give it a twirl.

The sun dips low, a fiery sight,
I'm still in chaos, with pure delight.
We leave the lake with tales to share,
A merry mishap, beyond compare.